Original title:
Stemmed Verses

Copyright © 2025 Creative Arts Management OÜ
All rights reserved.

Author: Vivian Laurent
ISBN HARDBACK: 978-1-80566-619-6
ISBN PAPERBACK: 978-1-80566-904-3

Inked in Green

In the garden of laughter, weeds grow tall,
Each with its own tale, absurdity for all.
A dandelion dances, a sunflower prances,
While broccoli whispers, 'Give me some chances!'

The carrot jokes to the cabbage on the side,
'We're rooted in this soil, with nowhere to hide!'
The radish chuckles, in a vibrant red dress,
'Life's more fun with a bit of a mess!'

The Poetry of Photosynthesis

Leaves like green pages, turning with grace,
Sipping on sunlight, in this leafy race.
Chlorophyll rhymes, in a dance of delight,
Giggles of nature, a feast every night.

Clouds in the sky, pull up a chair,
They muse on the ground, without a care.
Grass tickles toes, a verdant sitcom,
While flora plays strings, in a nature-born psalm.

Harvesting Harmony

The cornfield sings, with a swaying beat,
As pumpkins roll by, with laughter so sweet.
'Carve me a face,' calls the pumpkin with glee,
'Look at me shine, I'm the star of the spree!'

Ochre leaves tumble, in a whimsical race,
Fall's little giggles, an autumn embrace.
While apples debate, whose crunch is the best,
Each round little gem, in its fruity fest.

Nature's Metaphors

An acorn dreams big, of a towering fate,
While insects convene for a woodland debate.
'To fly or not to fly?' croaks the wise frog,
While a sloth yawns wide, in its leafy bog.

The wind tells the trees, silly secrets of cheer,
And mushrooms turn up, for a laugh and a beer.
With roots intertwined, in their quirky domain,
Nature's a stage, where absurd gets a reign.

Garden of Expression

In my garden of words, I do plant,
The daisies of jokes that make you chant.
With petunias of punchlines and humor to share,
Each bloom is a giggle, light as the air.

Weeding out sorrow, I laugh with delight,
Watering puns through day and the night.
Sunflowers dance, towering tall,
While I trip on my rhymes, and giggle and fall.

The Hum of Herbaceous Lines

In a patch of green, rhymes start to sprout,
Echoing laughter, that's what it's about.
Bees buzz with laughter, as I tell them a tale,
Of garden mishaps that never go stale.

The herbs all chime in, with leaves all a-flutter,
Thyme says I'm funny; Oregano's a nutter.
Chives chuckle softly with a fragrant snort,
While mint makes a joke of my fashion report.

Thorns and Thickets

In the midst of a thicket, I stumbled around,
Caught in a tangle, I fell to the ground.
The thorns they were prickly, but laughter was free,
As I tangled my words like a bush on a spree.

Brambles of banter grew wild and unkempt,
As I shared my exploits, a true mishap swept.
"Watch out for thorns!" a wildflower said bright,
"But that's where the fun is!" I laughed at my plight.

In the Shade of Stanzas

Beneath leafy verses where shadows play nice,
I write silly stanzas, like rolling a dice.
The sun peeks through laughter, a wink and a grin,
Where humor grows wild, let the fun times begin!

Sipping on rhymes, the cool breeze does cheer,
As I juggle my puns like a clown with no fear.
In the shade of my lines, creativity sways,
Each twist a new giggle, in so many ways.

Echoes of Growth

In a garden where the weeds dance,
A tomato wore a funny pants.
He strutted round with all his might,
Claiming he was ripe for the night.

The carrots giggled at his show,
While the lettuce hid from toe to toe.
The radish crackled with delight,
As veggies partied till the night.

Verses from the Vine

A grape once claimed, "I'm the best!"
With a crown of leaves atop his crest.
But when he stumbled on a rock,
He rolled away – oh, what a shock!

The ivy laughed from up above,
"You really need a little shove!"
The grape just laughed, then lost his way,
Spinning through the sunny day.

Blooms of Expression

A flower spoke with petals wide,
"Look at me! I'm full of pride!"
But when the wind began to blow,
She spun in circles saying, "Whoa!"

The bees all buzzed with laughter too,
As she twirled in her bright hue.
"Is it a dance, or just a fling?"
The daisies asked – the blooms took wing!

The Heart of a Bud

A tiny bud dreamed big and bold,
Wishing for stories yet untold.
But when he opened, what a sight,
His petals were a wild fright!

He laughed and said, "I do declare!"
"I'm just a bloom with messy hair!"
The garden giggled, what a spread,
For every bud, a smile ahead!

Draped in Dewdrops

Morning brings a splash of cheer,
Dewdrops dance like tiny spheres.
Grass tickles toes in early light,
Nature giggles, oh what a sight!

Ladybugs in hats so grand,
Hosting parties on the land.
Ants in suits, they march in line,
It's a bash, it's quite divine!

Butterflies with wings that blink,
Plotting mischief by the sink.
A worm with jokes, he steals the show,
Who knew that dirt could be aglow?

Sunshine laughs, it can't be beat,
As raindrops join in for a treat.
Every leaf a smile so bright,
Nature's whimsy, pure delight!

The Weave of Twigs

In the woods, where chatter sways,
Twigs tell tales of silly ways.
Squirrels prance with acorn hats,
Spinning yarns like cheeky brats.

Rabbits tap dance by the brook,
Turning pages in their book.
Frogs croak songs with zany flair,
Every hop's a special dare!

A wise old owl tries a joke,
But all he gets is silly smoke.
Branches bend and trees all grin,
Who knew the woods had such a spin?

Nature's stage, so full of glee,
Performers from the land and sea.
With every rustle, laugh, and cheer,
The twigs weave laughter far and near!

Lyrical Landscapes

Mountains hum a little tune,
Covered up in flowers' bloom.
Cacti play a prickly game,
With a wink, they stake their claim.

Rivers giggle, splashing bright,
Chasing fish that swim with flight.
Clouds have parties, bounce around,
While a rainbow sings, profound.

Every valley knows a jest,
Where even rocks can take a rest.
Lakes with puns that ripple wide,
Reflect the fun that cannot hide!

Fields of grass have ticklish fun,
With every breeze, they start to run.
Nature's laughter, free and bold,
Creating stories yet untold!

Growth Beyond Words

In the garden, plants confide,
Secrets of the world outside.
Veggies laugh with leafy smiles,
Sharing stories, stretching miles.

Flowers wear their blooming gear,
Telling puns, more than sincere.
Petals dance in sunny rays,
As roots conspire through the days.

A broccoli with jokes so green,
Makes even carrots join the scene.
Tomatoes giggle, round and red,
While pickles plot about their bread!

Growing tall with flair and glee,
The garden's ruckus, wild and free.
Every seed a giggle stirs,
There's growth, my friend, beyond mere words!

The Breath of Blossoms

In the garden, flowers yawn,
Petals wake with the dawn.
Bees buzz in a clumsy dance,
While daisies laugh at their chance.

Sunflowers wear hats quite tall,
They giggle at the garden's ball.
With bumblebees trying to strut,
One tripped on a rose, what a cut!

Tulips tell of wild dreams,
Whispering silly flower themes.
A daffodil lost its way,
Chased by rabbits at play.

In this quest for bloom and cheer,
Laughter springs from root to sphere.
Every bloom has tales to share,
With joy and fragrance in the air.

Verses of Verdancy

In the forest, the trees conspire,
With roots that twist like a liar.
Ferns flip and flop in a waltz,
While squirrels giggle at their faults.

Leaves giggle with a rustling sound,
As critters gambol all around.
A hedgehog rolls with flair tonight,
In the moon's glow, what a sight!

Bunnies hop and tell a joke,
While branches bend as if to poke.
A snail's slow crawl brings laughter near,
As he complains, 'Not again, oh dear!'

Every branch tells tales of fun,
In this green land beneath the sun.
Whispers dance on the gentle breeze,
Nature's laughter, sure to please.

Nature's Narratives

Once in a glade of golden hue,
A toad croaked lyrics, quite askew.
His frog friends laughed till they were blue,
'Your tone's a riot, but so untrue!'

A wise old owl, perched up high,
Said, 'Hoo, hoo! Give it a try!'
The fireflies joined in a glow,
As night wrapped them in a show.

Icicles dripped, making a sound,
That tickled the snow from the ground.
A bear danced, slipped on some ice,
With a grunt, 'Now that's not so nice!'

Every creature hums a tune,
As the stars giggle at the moon.
Nature's tales are quirky and bright,
Spreading laughter through the night.

Canopy Chronicles

In the treetops, monkeys prance,
Swinging 'round, they love to dance.
One lost his grip, oh what a scene,
Fell on a branch, but laughed between!

Parrots squawk with gossip loud,
As if they're the talk of the crowd.
'Did you hear about the snake's new hat?'
All critters chuckle, 'How about that!'

The wind tells stories with a sigh,
As leaves tell tales of days gone by.
A squirrel's leap brings quite the cheer,
With a nut in tow, he holds it dear.

From the canopy, laughter flows,
As nature's quirks continue to grow.
Each rustle and giggle leaves a trace,
In the wild, it's a funny place.

Flourishing Words

Words sprout up like weeds,
In gardens where laughter leads.
Each phrase a quirky bloom,
Spreading joy in every room.

Giggles twist and twine,
With puns that brightly shine.
A petal here, a joke there,
In this verbal garden fair.

Sunshine tickles the prose,
While charm in each line grows.
Let metaphors take flight,
In a playground of pure delight.

So let your verses laugh,
And dance like a busy calf.
For every pun and jest,
Is a seed of humor blessed.

Blossoms of the Mind

Thoughts flutter like bright fowl,
Chasing silliness and howl.
In the orchard of the wit,
Each quirk is a perfect fit.

Jokes bud on every branch,
In a whimsical word-dance.
Sprouts of laughter, sweet and rare,
Fill the air with fragrant flair.

Each idea, a cheery sprout,
Wrapping giggles all about.
With whimsy in every twist,
A merry thought's hard to resist.

So water those quirky dreams,
Let humor flow in streams.
In this garden wild and free,
Every laugh blooms joyfully!

Stalks of Soliloquy

Standing tall, the thoughts parade,
On stalks where silliness is laid.
Each soliloquy a tease,
Making grown-ups laugh with ease.

With witticisms strong and bright,
These stalks tickle, what a sight!
Words wobble, stiff yet spry,
In this funny flora high.

Chase the shadows, welcome sun,
With quips, our battles won.
Growling laughter, don't hold back,
In this patch of giggle knack.

Whispers wiggle through the air,
In this garden, no despair.
For every thought that slips and slides,
Laughter's where the silliness hides.

The Garden's Song

In the garden where we play,
Funny blooms lead the way.
Every joke a budding sprout,
Making butterflies scream out.

In the soil of laughter's grace,
Puns dance all around the place.
A chorus of chuckles rise,
Underneath the sunny skies.

Let the rhymes frolic anew,
With playful beats in every hue.
Here the garden sings with glee,
In every leaf, a jubilee.

So plant your words with whimsy's touch,
For laughter grows, oh so much.
In the music of delight,
Join the garden's song tonight!

Threads of Tranquility

In the garden, laughter grows,
With gnomes who dance in silly clothes.
The sun tickles the petals bright,
While ants march left, then take a flight.

A squirrel juggles acorns with flair,
As a frog croaks tunes from his chair.
Each breeze whispers a playful jest,
Nature's comedy at its best.

Tendrils of Thought

Thoughts twist like vines on a wall,
Some climb high, while others fall.
A bee buzzes jokes in the air,
With puns that tickle without a care.

The clouds giggle, shifting shapes,
A dinosaur that suddenly escapes.
Leaves rustle with secret glee,
As a snail wins a race, whee!

Roots and Rhythms

Roots tap-dance under dirt so deep,
Keeping secrets that they'll keep.
A worm in shades says, 'What's the fuss?'
While daisies debate who's the prettiest.

The rhythm shakes the trees awake,
A family of raccoons starts to shake.
With each branch waving, trees sway,
Nature's concert on full display.

The Language of Leaves

Leaves gossip in the rustling breeze,
Sharing tales with charming ease.
A potato rolls by, feeling grand,
Saying, 'I'm cooler than this sand!'

With cheeky chats and muddy feet,
The garden parties can't be beat.
While dandelions blow their fluff,
Claiming life's never really tough!

Roots in Rhyme

Beneath the soil they wriggle and giggle,
Roots arguing over who's grown the biggest.
They tickle the dirt and make it wiggle,
Claiming their space, oh, such a briskest!

With worms as their friends, they share silly tales,
Of raindrops that danced on their leafy sails.
Laughing at storms, they stand like gales,
Cracking jokes 'til the morning pales.

Petals of Thought

Petals are pondering life in bloom,
Wondering which way the wind will zoom.
With colors that blush in the sun's warm room,
They giggle at bees, avoiding their loom.

Conferring at dusk, they plan a parade,
"Let's confuse the deer, they'll be dismayed!"
With laughter and grace, they won't be delayed,
Making blossoms dance, oh, what a charade!

Whispering Stems

Stems stand tall, but they're secretly shy,
Whispering jokes that make leaves want to fly.
"Why did the grass blade let out a sigh?
Because it met a lawnmower, oh my!"

They chuckle together, swaying in glee,
Each sharing a tale of a hapless bee.
Their laughter erupts, oh, what jubilee,
In the garden where all feel so free!

The Language of Leaves

Leaves are conversing in soft, rustling tones,
Mixing up languages, like they're on phones.
"Did you hear that one 'bout the old garden gnomes?
They try to plant smiles, but grow squishy scones!"

With whispers of wind, they plot silly schemes,
Dreaming of picnics with mushrooms and creams.
Dancing with laughter, fulfilling their dreams,
These leaves sure are crafty, or so it seems!

Stanzas from the Seedbed

In the garden, seeds do dance,
With giggles caught in shady prance.
They sprout up tall, then tumble down,
Wearing dandelion crowns, not a frown.

Worms in bow ties perform their tricks,
As ladybugs do ballet flicks.
The carrots hum a jazzy tune,
While the radishes sway to the moon.

Sunflowers strike a silly pose,
As broccoli giggles and tickles their toes.
Bees are buzzing in a wild spree,
Crafting honey like a comedy.

So come one, come all, to this wild show,
Where every plant has its own glow.
In the seedbed, laughter takes root,
Growing joy that's oh-so-astute.

Cadence of the Canes

Bamboo sways in the playful breeze,
Tickling the clouds, oh what a tease!
They whisper jokes to the passing winds,
While crickets join in, a symphony begins.

A sugar cane jokes about being sweet,
Says he's the life of every treat.
But when he gets too close to a knife,
He cracks a smirk on the edge of life.

Tall reeds play tag along the shore,
Giggling as they lean and soar.
They tickle fish as they pass by,
In the cadence of the reeds, oh my!

So let's sway with the canes tonight,
Embracing laughter till the morning light.
In this rhythm, we find our cheer,
With every rustle, joy comes near.

Verses of Verdure

The lawn is laughing in shades of green,
Jokes about weeds, oh what a scene!
Grass-blades whisper in cheerful tones,
While daisies toss their petals like stones.

The ferns do a jig, all spruced and proud,
Swinging their fronds in a leafy crowd.
The violets giggle when no one's around,
Saying, "We're the best blooms in town!"

Moss plays the role of a wise old sage,
Telling tales of plants on every page.
"Keep your roots deep, and your humor high,
We're the green jesters, oh me, oh my!"

So stroll through the garden, enjoy the spree,
Nature's comedy is wild and free.
In the verses of verdure, we find delight,
Laughter grows well in the soft moonlight.

Spun from Saplings

Tiny saplings are known to jest,
With branches waving, they're at their best.
They wear acorn hats and leafy clothes,
And tell tall tales that nobody knows.

One charming oak shows off its height,
Claiming it can reach the stars at night.
While the willows sway and tease the breeze,
Singing soft songs among the trees.

The baby pines poke fun at the sun,
"Bet you can't outshine our green fun!
We're the future, with so much zest,
In this big forest, we're truly blessed!"

So let's frolic with these playful sprigs,
In a world where laughter always digs.
Saplings remind us, as we twirl and spin,
Joy is the root that grows from within.

Reaching for the Sky

I saw a tree with arms so wide,
To hug the clouds and take a ride.
It whispered jokes to passing birds,
And laughed at all the silly words.

Its branches danced like crazy hats,
When squirrels jumped like acrobats.
I joined the fun, we had a blast,
The sky was blue, the time flew fast.

The tree giggled with every breeze,
It entertained the buzzing bees.
With every twist, another joke,
That left us all in merry yoke.

I stretched my arms, I felt so bold,
To reach the heights, or so I'm told.
But laughter's gravity pulled me down,
With a silly, leaf-shaped crown.

The Lattice of Life

In a garden maze of tangled vines,
A ladybug wore polka-dots, fine!
She claimed the leaves were quite a stage,
For all the bugs who love to rage.

With beetles drumming on the ground,
And caterpillars twirling round.
They staged a play called 'All That Rusts',
With a chorus of whimsical gusts.

A snail, dressed up like a king,
Declared it time for a bug to sing!
They laughed and spun in pure delight,
Under the stars, oh what a sight!

The lattice shook with joy so loud,
The petals bounced, the leaves were proud!
And as the night began to wane,
All tangled up, they danced in vain.

Timeless Trunks

There are trunks that stand like ancient kings,
With tales to weave from feathered things.
They share their secrets with the wind,
While curious critters race and spin.

One trunk declared it was a time machine,
To the past where all was green!
It spun a yarn that's quite absurd,
Of why the chicken crossed, I've heard!

"To reach the silly, silly worm!"
It chuckled loud, began to squirm.
From knots and grooves, it made us laugh,
With puns about the nature's path.

So here's to trunks with jokes to spare,
That stand so tall, beyond compare!
While we all giggle at their pranks,
For laughter flows from forest ranks!

The Sigh of Leaves

Oh, the leaves in autumn take a breath,
And fall to ground like whispers, death.
They joke and jive on paths so clear,
As children laugh, full of cheer.

"Catch me quick!" a leaf would shout,
As wind helped it twist about.
They danced in pairs, a waltzing spree,
In colors bright, just wait and see!

But what's the trick, we all do ask,
To be so free, oh leaf, that's your task?
They chuckled soft, "Be bold, be bright,
Life's just a game, enjoy the flight!"

And as the boughs let go their treasure,
The sigh of leaves was purest pleasure.
With each soft grip, their laughter flew,
As all the world turned golden too.

Enchanted by the Earth

The grass wore shoes of dew, my friend,
A fashion trend that won't quite end.
Earthworms weave dreams beneath the bed,
While daisies giggle, 'Look! We're fed!'

The sun plays peek-a-boo with clouds,
While the squirrels throw acorn crowds.
Rabbits hop like they own the street,
Saying, 'Watch our dance, it's oh so neat!'

Petal-Powered Verses

Dandelions blow like fuzzy dreams,
While bees do the cha-cha, or so it seems.
The tulips gossip about the bees,
'Did you see his dance? Oh, such a tease!'

A rose complains of thorny woes,
While violets tease with gentle prose.
'Let's paint the garden in laughs and cheer!'
'A flower pun a day keeps worries clear!'

The Boughs of Expression

Oh, the branches wave like they just don't care,
Sharing secrets with the breeze up there.
The owls hoot jokes at the break of dawn,
While squirrels plot pranks on the folks who yawn.

The pines recite poetry in the night,
With needles sharp but hearts so light.
'Let's twist and shout, with roots so deep!'
'And remind the world, we're not here to weep!'

Colorful Canopies

Under canopies of crimson and gold,
Trees tell stories that never get old.
Leaves shimmy down in autumn's dance,
While branches wiggle, given the chance.

A rainbow of colors spills on the ground,
While mushrooms giggle, 'A party we've found!'
Beneath the arch, the frogs sing a song,
'Join our ribbit raves, come dance along!'

Flourish Through The Lines

In a garden where whispers bloom,
Funny plants are making room.
Roses giggle, daisies dance,
With each petal, a comical chance.

Thyme jokes that he's on the run,
While mint insists it's all in fun.
They plant their feet, roots deep down,
Wearing nature's finest crown.

Sunflowers bow with silly grace,
Chasing sunbeams in this space.
The wind tells tales of laughter bright,
Underneath the moonlit night.

So join the green laugh-out-loud spree,
Where every leaf wants to be free.
In this silly, thriving vine,
We'll flourish through each goofy line.

The Tapestry of Twigs

A tapestry woven with stories told,
Of skits and pranks, a wonder to behold.
Twigs with giggles, branches in glee,
They twist and turn, they dance so free.

Behold the oak, he strokes his beard,
With each breeze, a joke is cheered.
Cedar cackles, "Watch me sway!"
While willow whispers, "Merry play!"

Together they weave a silly scene,
With acorns rolling, a laughter machine.
Redwood chuckles, wise and profound,
In this funny forest, joy abounds.

So gather 'round this merry patch,
Where nature's jests are sure to catch.
In every gnarled twist and turn,
The tapestry of laughter will always burn.

The Embrace of Earth

Earth hugs tight with a comical grin,
Every creature feels the spin.
Mushrooms bob in a goofy dance,
While ants march on, lost in a trance.

The soil cracks jokes, quite underground,
"Mind the roots, or you'll fall down!"
Worms tumble in a messy heap,
Whispering secrets, they cannot keep.

Grasshoppers leap with silly flair,
Landing in flowers without a care.
The sun shines bright, a golden cheer,
As earth chuckles, "Stay close, my dear!"

So let's celebrate this funny sphere,
Where nature's humor is always near.
In every nook and cranny, we see,
An embrace of laughter, wild and free.

Swaying Echoes

Echoes of laughter in gentle sway,
Trees chuckling as the winds play.
Branches wave in a jolly tease,
Tickling the air with the greatest ease.

Leaves whispering secrets, full of cheer,
"Follow us, come dance, my dear!"
The breeze brings stories from afar,
About a squirrel, a rising star.

Each rustle a giggle, each snap a jest,
Nature's humor never takes a rest.
The shadows play hide and seek,
In this forest, it's fun we seek.

So sway along with the echoes bright,
Where joy and laughter take flight.
In this realm of mirth and glee,
Join the chorus of nature's spree.

Scripted in Soil

In the garden, plants recite,
Whispered jokes in morning light.
The daisies giggle, the roses snort,
While the weeds just dance, a wild sport.

Tulips tweet about their dress,
Caught in the breeze, they must confess.
Sunflowers sway in silly prance,
As the bumblebees join the dance.

Flora-Fueled Dreams

A cabbage dreams of acting roles,
In a vegetable show, it plays the soles.
The carrots joke about their height,
While leeks boast of a fancy bite.

Petunias paint their petals bright,
Dreaming of fame, shining in the light.
Lavender can't stop making puns,
Tickling bees and having fun.

Blooming Connections

The violets chat about the weather,
With lilies laughing, all come together.
Dandelions blowing wishes late,
Each wish a laugh—oh, isn't it great?

Roses roll their eyes at thorny tales,
While ferns tell tales of epic fails.
In the heart of the garden, joy expands,
With laughter shared in leafy bands.

Seeds of Thought

In a packet where ideas sprout,
Each seed a jest, no room for doubt.
Puns grow tall from the ground below,
While laughter seeds the soil, you know.

Compost bins filled with wisdom old,
Feed the jokes—become quite bold.
Sprouting dreams in a silly way,
Growing giggles day by day.

Grafted Dreams

In the orchard, trees all wear hats,
One is a pear, the other a cat.
They argue 'bout fruit, oh what a surprise,
A melon in spring? What a whimsical prize.

Roots exchange whispers, content in the dirt,
A gopher plays poker, for what it's worth.
Twigs throw confetti, the leaves dance with glee,
While worms write their novels, "Best-Sellers" you see!

Beneath the Bark

Squirrels stockpiling acorns, quite the sight,
They bicker, they laugh till the fall of the night.
A raccoon steals donuts, oh what a crime,
While bees start a band, oh so sweet in their rhyme.

A sly little fox in a tuxedo so neat,
Dances with shadows, oh how they compete.
Branches join wildly, like dancers in trance,
Nature's own party, it's a wild, crazy dance!

Tales from the Thicket

In thickets so thick, where the jokes come alive,
Lizards wear glasses, the chameleons dive.
They tell tales of old, with a flick of their tails,
As frogs croak in chorus, with laughter that sails.

The owls hoot in tune, such a wisecrack crew,
While hedgehogs roll laughter, and play peek-a-boo.
Each bush has a secret, a pun waiting there,
In the heart of the wild, giggles fill the air.

In the Arms of Vines

Vines twist and twirl, they shimmy and sway,
With cucumbers laughing at cabbages' play.
A tomato throws shade at a corn stalk so tall,
While peppers sit snickering, in a good-natured brawl.

In trellises' embrace, they share all their dreams,
Of veggies in helmets, bursting at the seams.
As carrots wear shades, in the sun they recline,
A salad of laughter, all squared up in fine wine!

Essence Blooming

In a garden where daisies play,
A dandelion danced, come what may,
With a jaunty hat made of sun,
Declared, "Look at me, I'm number one!"

Butterflies giggled, flowers joined in,
As the breeze shared jokes with a spin,
A tulip winked, a daffodil swayed,
In this wild party, no one's delayed.

The sun blushed, wearing golden rays,
While bees buzzed tunes in funny ways,
Each petal a laugh, each leaf a sigh,
Nature's comedy, oh my, oh my!

At dusk, the crickets began to croon,
Under the watch of a curious moon,
The garden giggled, the plants took a bow,
In this essence of joy, we all say wow!

Imprints of the Earth

Footprints of worms dance in the dirt,
A snail in a race with dreams to flirt,
Mice hold tiny parties near the trees,
While ants chant tales on warm summer breeze.

Rabbits wearing hats made of leaves,
Play hopscotch while the world deceives,
Toads croak jokes, frogs laugh in delight,
Each creature at play from day until night.

Textures of soil where stories unfold,
Tales of the critters in whispers bold,
Mounds create mics for the shyer ones,
Earth's silent laughs sparkle like fun guns.

As the sun sets, the giggles will last,
Earth's merry chorus of nature so vast,
In every footprint, a giggle we find,
In the dance of the earth, we're all intertwined.

The Symphony of Stems

In the symphony where stems do sway,
Each one sings in its own funny way,
A broccoli tree with dreams of ballet,
While carrots dream of a Broadway play.

The conductor, a wise old garden gnome,
With a leaf for a baton, brings joy home,
Mozart's tunes bounce from green to brown,
While beans bop along in a leafy gown.

Sunflowers bow, the violets hum,
Together they march in a silly drum,
Radishes tap dance while peas do the twist,
Can you believe that you might have missed?

As dusk falls, the critters take heed,
They replace the music with giggles indeed,
Nature's own band, in the night so bright,
In this sweet symphony, we find pure delight.

Verdant Visions

In a patch of green where dreams collide,
Tiny sprouts share secrets they hide,
A beet in a bowtie tells silly jokes,
While chard and spinach giggle like folks.

The daisies parade with petals of pride,
While twirling around in nature's wide stride,
Even the weeds join this riotous spree,
Saying, "We're not just bad, we're quirky, you see!"

The sun winks at clouds with a grin,
It knows the mischief that waits to begin,
As light dapples down on this funny scene,
Every leaf rustles like laughter unseen.

When twilight arrives, the dreams take flight,
Blending with the stars in a dance of light,
In verdant visions where joy surely lives,
Nature's own laughter is all that it gives.

The Dance of Daisies

In a field where flowers sway,
Daisies twist in bright array.
They wear hats made of sun,
And shout, "Oh, what fun!"

Bees do a comical jig,
Buzzing loud, oh so big.
They trip on petals wide,
And laugh as they glide.

The daisies wink and prance,
Inviting all to dance.
With stems that twist and twirl,
They spin and happily whirl.

So come and join the spree,
In this garden jubilee.
With daisies all aglow,
Let's dance like there's no snow!

Rhymes of the Canopy

In the forest, leaves play tricks,
With whispers and funny kicks.
Squirrels write poems in trees,
While birds chirp with giggles and wheezes.

The branches sway to the beat,
While acorns bounce on their feet.
Oh look, a raccoon in a hat,
Singing high, isn't he fat?

The sun peeks through with a laugh,
As shadows take their photograph.
A dance-off breaks out with flair,
The whole canopy joins with care.

With rhythm and cheer we explore,
Every branch, we can't ignore.
Underneath the leafy dome,
We find a funny place called home.

Blossoms Beneath the Moon

Underneath the moon's soft glow,
Petals giggle, putting on a show.
The tulips wear their crowns of night,
While lilies dance in pure delight.

A butterfly slips on a sock,
And gives the roses quite a shock.
With every twirl and funny flap,
They spin around like in a nap!

Crickets join with tiny tunes,
Strumming strings under the moons.
Jasmine sways and hums along,
Together they sing a silly song.

So come and see this flowery laugh,
Where petals grow and giggles half.
In the garden where dreams bloom,
Let's dance and sweep away the gloom!

Harmony in the Hedge

In hedges thick where critters meet,
A hedgehog taps his tiny feet.
The rabbits giggle, tails in the air,
While they hop without a care.

The snails are slow, but bring the beat,
With tiny drums made from little feet.
The hedgehog spins and takes a bow,
While bushes cheer, "Oh wow!"

A fox with sunglasses wanders by,
Sipping tea as he lets out a sigh.
"Isn't life so very grand?"
The badgers clap their little hands!

Each critter joins in, full of cheer,
Creating joy we hold so dear.
In the hedges, under the glow,
Let's laugh together and watch joy flow!

Palettes of Petals

In gardens where the daisies dance,
Colors clash and take a chance.
The roses giggle, bright and red,
While violets plot from their garden bed.

Tulips twirl in silly lines,
Wiggling stems like playful vines.
Sunflowers grin with faces wide,
While buttercups play hide and slide.

Dandelions puff and blow,
Sneaky wishes, don't you know?
Petals laugh, a vibrant cheer,
In this dance, we find no fear!

So grab a brush, a splash of hue,
Join the blooms—a merry crew!
With every petal, giggles bloom,
In a garden of laughter, bright like a room.

The Harmony of Harvest

In fields where veggies slap and cheer,
Carrots chuckle, 'We're all here!'
Potatoes roll and cheer them on,
While onions weep, but sing a song.

Corn whispers jokes, in rows so tall,
Zucchini laughs, it's having a ball.
Tomatoes blush, but join the fun,
Cucumbers giggle under the sun.

Beans climb high, they steal the show,
With leafy tricks, they steal the grow.
A pumpkin grins, round and bright,
'The more we harvest, the more delight!'

In this patch of jolly beings,
The laughter echoes in their leanings.
Together they sway, a silly sight,
In harmony, they take their flight!

The Ink of Nature

In a forest filled with crafty pens,
Trees scribble tales of playful friends.
Squirrels plot with acorn might,
While owls hoot, 'It's time for flight!'

The brook giggles, it flows with glee,
Writing ripples in a dance, you see.
Mushrooms gather, their caps all bright,
As the fireflies provide the light.

Each leaf sings, a note so sweet,
Nature's ink makes stories complete.
With every twist, and every bend,
It's laughter that the wild ones send.

In this book where shadows play,
Pages turn in a breezy way.
So grab a quill, and write with cheer,
In nature's script, we hold so dear!

Roots and Rhythms

Down below where secrets creep,
Roots tell tales while the soil sleeps.
Wiggly worms make goofy sounds,
As laughter bubbles through the grounds.

Tiny critters hold a jam,
With rhythms like a grand old fam.
Beetles tap with tiny feet,
While ants march along the beat.

Mushrooms sway to earthy tunes,
Bouncing high like happy balloons.
The grass blades shimmy in a line,
As nature grooves with herbal wine.

So join the roots beneath the earth,
Dance along with all their mirth.
In this rhythm of whirls and spins,
The laughter blooms as nature grins!

The Woven Wilderness

In the forest where squirrels play,
They weave their acorn hats each day.
With branches tickling their furry tails,
They dance on logs like tiny gales.

The birds gossip high in the trees,
About the latest nutty cheese.
While rabbits hop with silly grace,
They giggle as they join the race.

The brook babbles jokes in the night,
While the fireflies flicker their light.
Each creature cracks up, oh what a sight,
In this wild world of pure delight.

A bear joins in with a hefty cheer,
Telling tales with a voice so clear.
In the woven wild, laughter is found,
Where joy and mischief abound around.

Flourish and Fable

In gardens where the daisies sway,
The gnomes hold parades on sunny days.
With flower hats and rhymes to share,
They spin tall tales of velvet air.

The bees buzz in their silly suits,
Dancing round like they're in loopy boots.
While butterflies flaunt their vibrant wings,
Playing tag and doing silly things.

The sunflowers watch and shake their heads,
As catnip plants act like they're in beds.
They laugh at the chaos, the joy in bloom,
In this fable garden, there's always room.

At night, the stars twinkle in delight,
As owls hoot jokes till the morning light.
In tales where laughter perpetually flows,
The world's a stage for all that grows.

Verses in the Wind

The wind whispers jokes to the trees,
Tickling branches with playful ease.
Leaves giggle and flutter with glee,
As the breeze dances wild and free.

Dandelions shout with poofy heads,
While tumbleweeds roll over beds.
Clouds chuckle as they drift and glide,
Sharing secrets with the countryside.

The kite on its string performs a show,
With flips and tricks that steal the glow.
A gust lifts it, soaring so high,
Like dreams that tickle and want to fly.

In verses spun by the playful swirl,
Nature's laughter makes the heart twirl.
With whispers of joy, they surely send,
A melody of mirth, a splendid trend.

Echoes Among the Evergreens

Among the pines where the echoes call,
A raccoon tells jokes, making all fall.
The owls laugh deep in the night,
While shadows dance in the pale moonlight.

Evergreens chuckle, standing so tall,
With needles that shimmer, they join the brawl.
As squirrels debate who's the best acorn,
Their laughter wakes creatures of thorn.

Beneath the stars, mischief takes flight,
As crickets chirp through the cool night.
Frogs join with ribbits that sound like glee,
A symphony played in the woodland spree.

In this forest, humor flows like a stream,
Where every creature fits in the theme.
An echo of laughter, so rich, so bright,
In the evergreens' arms, it feels just right.

Rhythm of the Roots

In the garden, weeds can dance,
Twisting, twirling, given a chance.
The carrots sing, the peas will sway,
As worms bust moves, hip-hop all day.

With onions laughing, tears on cue,
They tell the jokes, oh what a crew!
A silly squash, with a hat so tall,
Declares himself the king of them all.

Tomatoes giggle, they can't keep still,
Rolling 'round, it's quite a thrill.
As radishes wear their brightest red,
Making all the greens feel misled.

In this plot, a party so grand,
With every veggie taking their stand.
So grab a fork, join the fun,
Let's eat and laugh, till day is done!

The Pulse of Petals

On petals soft, the bees do hum,
While daisies cheer, 'Come take a seat!'
A rose with thorns jokes, 'Don't be glum!
Just don't get too close, I'm quite a feat!'

The sunflowers pose, striking a glare,
'We're the models of the flower fair!'
While violets whisper, 'We're shy but bold,
Our secrets of beauty never told.'

A lavender's giggle floats on the breeze,
Tickling the tulips, oh what a tease!
With every bloom, a prank they play,
In this garden, it's laughter all day.

Petals flutter with joy and mirth,
Spreading smiles all over the earth.
So join this dance, skip and twirl,
In the scents of fun, let laughter unfurl!

Verse Nestled in Leaves

Inside the leaves, a secret space,
Where critters frolic, a sweet embrace.
A squirrel in shades plays peek-a-boo,
While birds recite a funny haiku.

With rustling leaves, they make a band,
Drumming on acorns, perfectly planned.
While chattering chipmunks take a turn,
Telling tales of nuts they yearn.

Each leaf a page, each branch a stage,
The wind is the laughter, they all engage.
A concert of chirps, a giggle or two,
In this leafy world, fun is the glue.

So next time you wander, take a peek,
At the leafy verses, so unique!
Join the critters, hear their song,
In the forest's heart, where we all belong!

Lush Lyrics

In a meadow where daisies sway,
The grasshoppers dance, come join the play.
'What's the best part of a sunny day?'
They chirp and hop, with humor in gray.

Butterflies flutter, wearing their best,
Whispering jokes, putting smiles to the test.
A bumblebee buzzes, full of cheek,
Saying, 'Life's too sweet if you don't sneak!'

The clovers chuckle, four leaves apiece,
Sharing their luck, never to cease.
While daisies giggle, in white and gold,
Telling stories that never get old.

So dance with the flowers, twirl round and round,
In the rhythm of laughter, joy can be found.
With lush lyrics filling the air,
Life's funnier when you just don't care!

Fragments of Flora

In the garden, plants like to talk,
Ferns gossip 'bout the bold old oak.
Petunias wear hats made of dew,
While daisies chuckle, sharing a view.

Roses and thorns are best of friends,
With teasing jokes that never end.
A sunflower spins in a silly dance,
While weeds invite ants for a chance.

Tulips wear sneakers, what a sight!
They race with the wind, feeling light.
Lettuce retorts, "I'm winning this race!"
Oh, nature's bloom has such a grace!

A garden party opens wide,
With bees as guests, none can hide.
The veggies laugh, it's quite the spree,
In this funny patch, wild and free.

Rhythms of the Orchard

In the orchard, apples play tag,
Chasing the wind, a little snag.
Pears giggle, stacked in a row,
While cherries gossip, just for show.

Plums wear sunglasses under the sun,
Yelling, "Look at us, aren't we fun?"
Oranges roll, having a ball,
As squirrels debate who's most tall.

Each fruit sings a tune so sweet,
With melodies that can't be beat.
The branches sway in joyful glee,
As nature hums a silly spree.

When autumn comes, the jokes don't stop,
Pumpkins join in, ready to hop.
While cider flows, laughter is rife,
In this orchard, humor is life!

Layers of Lyrical Life

Beneath the surface, worms compose,
Verses about the soil that grows.
Each grain of dirt sings its own tune,
As crickets chirp under the moon.

The roots hold secrets, twisting tight,
Sharing whispers with all their might.
Leaves tell stories of wild escapades,
While shadows play in leafy shades.

In this world, each layer shines,
With laughter hiding in the vines.
From blossoms bold to roots below,
Life's a stage, putting on a show.

With every season, humor grows,
Nature writing its own prose.
In layers deep, the fun unfolds,
A lyrical tale that never grows old!

Sprouts of Serenity

Sprouts giggle as they rise from ground,
Bouncing up with a silly sound.
They share their dreams of reaching the sky,
Swapping tales as butterflies fly.

In morning dew, they play a game,
A racing match of budding fame.
Sunbeams tickle their leafy cheeks,
As they burst forth in playful streaks.

Each small green shoot has jokes to tell,
Dancing with joy, oh, isn't it swell?
Nature's laughter fills the air,
With sprightly sprouts beyond compare.

In fields of laughter, they stand tall,
Giving cheer to one and all.
Even the shadows join their cheer,
In this world, fun is always near!

Fragments of Flora

In a garden of giggles and gaffes,
The daisies wear their silly laughs.
Roses blushing in a mock parade,
Tulips dancing in a happy cascade.

Bees buzzing with jokes in flight,
While mushrooms play cards in the night.
Even the weeds have their own cheer,
Winking at flowers, 'You're looking queer!'

Violets chuckle at their own hue,
Saying, 'Who knew we'd play peekaboo?'
The ferns whisper tales of their past,
With roots that tangle and laughter that lasts.

So let's frolic in this plant-based jest,
Where humor blooms and we're all guests.
Nature's comedy, a verdant spree,
Come join the fun, it's all free!

Petals in the Breeze

Petals flit around like butterflies,
With pollen jokes twinkling in their eyes.
A daffodil slips on a dew drop,
While laughing sunflowers can't seem to stop.

The breeze tickles leaves like it's a game,
"Catch me if you can!" it shouts with fame.
Chlorophyll giggles at the tale of time,
As ants climb trees in a conga line.

Lilies ponder why frogs get the croaks,
While daisies share puns, all in good folks.
A riot of colors joins in the cheer,
"Who planted these jokes? We need them here!"

So dance with the petals, swirl in delight,
As nature spins tales from morning to night.
In this floral frolic, there's never a bore,
Each petal's a punchline, forevermore!

Echoes of the Earth

Echoes bounce through the leafy glade,
Trees whisper secrets in a leafy braid.
The moss chuckles at the world so vast,
Reminding us all of our childhood blast.

Rocks giggle softly under their mulch,
While crickets chirp with a crooked lurch.
The soil sings songs of seeds sprouting news,
Every kernel knows just what to choose.

Clouds play hide-and-seek with the sun,
While shadows and light engage in their fun.
The wind blows laughter from the top of a hill,
With echoes that dance and never stand still.

In the chorus of nature, a laugh we find,
In every rustle, we are all intertwined.
So let us listen, let the giggles resound,
In the heart of the earth, joy knows no bound!

Verdant Verses

In a patch of green where giggles grow,
The ferns and ivy put on a show.
Grasshoppers dance in synchronized glee,
While daisies spin tales of who they could be.

The trees crack jokes in rustling leaves,
Making even the wind contemplate reprieves.
Peonies puff out their petals with pride,
Competing with tulips, side by side.

A squirrel shares riddles from atop a branch,
Dropping acorns like seeds in a chance.
The sunbeams chuckle at shadows they cast,
As laughter in greens makes days fly past.

So join this jolly green, a playful trend,
Where every plant's a quirky friend.
In verdant verses, humor takes root,
In nature's embrace, laughter's pursuit!

Utterances of the Garden

The carrots whispered low, a tale of woe,
As lettuce giggled, swaying to and fro.
Bees buzzed with laughter, a busy parade,
While daisies danced lightly, unafraid.

Rabbits cracked jokes, all ears in the row,
With radishes blushing, sporting a glow.
A sunflower shrugged, 'Life's just a game!'
While marigolds snickered, calling her name.

The wind joined the fun, bringing laughter around,
As weeds, feeling cheeky, started to clown.
And so in the patch, with a pop and a twist,
The garden erupted in laughter not missed.

Yet one solemn cactus, all prickly and dry,
Declared with a sigh, "What's all this, why?"
But everyone giggled, the blooms all agreed,
A garden's best moments are in laughter indeed.

Sprout Shadows

In the soil, secrets hide, sprouting up in glee,
A tiny pea pod peeked, shouting, "Look at me!"
While grasshoppers chirped, playing tag with the sun,
And ants held a concert, oh what a fun run!

Petunias were posh, in their colorful hats,
While daisies debated who topped the best sprats.
A sunflower chimed in, "I'm tallest, you see!"
But roses just chuckled, "Well, that's not key!"

Down by the roots, the worms had a ball,
Telling tales of the rain, with the best of them all.
Laughing at puddles, just splashing about,
"The world's much more fun when you're not filled with doubt!"

So in this green world, where shadows twirl bright,
The laughter of blooms fills each day and each night.
Nature's own comedy, writ large and unfurled,
Sprout shadows abound, in this whimsical world.

Lyrical Tangles

Twisted vines frolic in the warm afternoon,
Singing songs of sunshine, to a cheerful tune.
A butterfly winked, with a flurry of flair,
While the ivy, in laughter, tangled her hair.

"Hang on!" said the rose, "I've gotten quite stuck!"
The thorns giggled softly, "Oh what rotten luck!"
A daffodil chortled, "What a sight on this day!"
As petals all chuckled, in a tangled ballet.

Underneath all the fun, the frogs croaked a beat,
Joking about ants that they just couldn't meet.
"What's hopping?" they crooned, with a wink and a grin,
For laughter's the treasure they always win.

A bumblebee buzzed, making rounds with delight,
Saying, "Joke's on you, I'm a bee out of sight!"
And in lyrical tangles, the flora would swirl,
Where giggles and glee make the garden unfurl.

The Pulse of Petals

At dawn, the flowers woke with a yawn and a stretch,
Each petal with rhythm, making nature's sketch.
The daisies started tapping, a dance on the ground,
While tulips joined in with a giggling sound.

"Let's twirl!" cried the violets, all tossed in a spin,
While zinnias clapped while the fun would begin.
A chorus of blossoms, a whimsical cheer,
The pulse of the petals rang out far and near.

In the middle of this joy, the bugs flitted fast,
With ladybugs laughing, their worries surpassed.
And the sun just smiled down, all golden and warm,
As blossoms kept bouncing, embracing the charm.

A wind-swept surprise, the blooms took to flight,
With petals a-flutter, they danced through the night.
The pulse of the petals, a party in bloom,
In the garden of laughter, there's always more room.

The Orchard's Overture

In the garden, apples giggle,
Oranges roll, their laughter wiggle.
A pear named Pete told a pun so sweet,
The tree barked back, tapping its feet.

Cherries chase in a fruity race,
While lemons pout, making a face.
Plums in pajamas, ready in style,
Swing and sway, making the crowd smile.

Bees buzz jokes, around they swirl,
While peaches dance, giving a twirl.
The sun smiles down, the grass gets up,
Mixing up fun in a juice-filled cup.

So gather 'round for fruity cheer,
With jokes and jests that bring us near.
The orchard's tunes, a joyous cheer,
Nature's giggle, a dance so clear.

Budding Imaginations

Seeds whisper wishes under the ground,
Dreams sprout legs and start to bound.
Petals wear hats, oh what a sight,
While vines play hopscotch, full of delight.

A daisy named Daisy thought she could fly,
With dreams so big she nearly touched the sky.
But winds were tricky, playing a game,
She tumbled and giggled, but never felt shame.

Roots weave stories, enacting a play,
Where carrots complain about old radish gray.
Beet roots roll for the comedy role,
While broccoli broods, but deep down is whole.

In this patch of whimsy, no worries abound,
Each sprout and leaf in laughter is found.
They dream as they grow, a joyous parade,
In the garden of giggles, where fun never fades.

The Feel of Ferns

Ferns fluffed up, with spiky hair,
Doing the twist without a care.
A lizard lounges, thinking it grand,
While snails take bets on the slippery stand.

Leaves tickle toes that stroll by slow,
In this green jungle, it's a lively show.
Chirping frogs croon a tune so fine,
While dandelions laugh over some wine.

Moss creates pillows for the tired feet,
As ants march on, in a pattern neat.
Squirrels gossip about hidden nuts,
While wildflowers chuckle, and shake their guts.

Under the shade, it's a restful scene,
Nature's laughter flows like a dream.
The feel of ferns, a whispering delight,
Keeps the spirits dancing, day and night.

Melodies of the Meadow

In the meadow, grass sings a song,
With daisies dancing, they all sing along.
Butterflies flutter, a colorful swirl,
Tickling the air as the wind starts to twirl.

A hare on a hop lost his shoe,
With a laugh and a smile, he gives it a cue.
The frogs are the chorus, a ribbiting crew,
While bees buzz the beat, yes, that's how they do!

Cows join the band with a moo and a sway,
Creating a rhythm that brightens the day.
The sun plays a tune, shining so bright,
As the meadow's delight blossoms in light.

With a wink and a giggle, they celebrate well,
Nature's own party, with stories to tell.
So come join the fun at this joyous show,
Where the melodies flow, and the laughter will grow.

When Roots Speak

When roots decide to chat, they giggle,
They tickle worms and tease the wiggle.
With every whisper, dirt shakes and sighs,
While leaves above snicker, oh my, oh my!

The carrots claim they're wise and bold,
While onions cry, 'We're never sold!'
In this underground party, laughter does flow,
With glee and fun that only plants know.

The daisies roll their eyes in glee,
As radishes dance with gnarled feet.
Roots share old tales of the rainy day,
And secrets of sunlight that went astray.

In the soil, a joke gets passed around,
Over bare feet chasing soft ground.
When roots speak, oh what a scene,
Nature's comedy, lively and keen!

Nature's Silent Symphony

In the garden, silence breaks, it bends,
When nature plays, with laughter, it sends.
A worm on a lute brings tunes alive,
While flowers twirl, oh how they strive!

The breeze hums softly, a mischievous tune,
While mushrooms dance under silver moon.
A chorus of crickets and frogs take flight,
Nature's sweet tune, such a joyous sight!

Each rustle of leaves has a rhythm and beat,
As squirrels shimmy on happy little feet.
The tulips giggle, their petals unfold,
In this silent symphony, stories are told.

Who knew that nature held this much cheer?
A raucous melody, oh my dear!
As laughter swells beneath the bright sky,
Nature's antics will never say die!

Thorns and Threnodies

In a garden where thorns play the lead,
They poke fun, oh yes, that's their creed.
With jesting jabs and pricks they parade,
Each thorn a joke, in their sharp charade.

The roses complain, 'Must you be so sly?'
'We're just blooming, oh give us a try!'
But thorns just chuckle, with humor so sharp,
As they strum their pain like a catchy harp.

A cactus cracks jokes about desert heat,
While violets chuckle, feeling quite sweet.
Each bloom shakes its head, in mock despair,
Thorns and threnodies fill the air!

Together they weave a tale so absurd,
In this prickly hilarity, laughter is stirred.
Nature's jesters, all bitter and bright,
In the garden of wit, they shine day and night!

Whispered Secrets from the Soil

In the cool of the earth, whispers abound,
Rustling secrets that dance all around.
A peanut jokes, 'I'm buried too deep!'
While onions giggle, they just can't keep!

"Do you hear the stories the earth likes to tell?"
Chortles the lettuce, feeling quite swell.
"I heard a flower bragging about its flair,"
Said a shy little sprout, with roots in its hair.

The mushrooms snicker, 'We see it all here,
From the ants' tiny tales to the bug's wild cheer.'
In darkness, they chuckle, oh such a sight,
Soil's funny gossip, bubbling with light!

As whispers resound and the laughter increases,
In the heart of the earth, the humor never ceases.
From the smallest seed to the tallest tree,
In nature's loud laughter, we all agree!

www.ingramcontent.com/pod-product-compliance
Lightning Source LLC
Chambersburg PA
CBHW051645160426
43209CB00004B/803